Stage 4 Pack A

Floppy's Phonics
Fiction

Kate Ruttle

Group/Guided Re

Contents

Introduction	2
Phonic focus	3
Vocabulary	4
Comprehension strategies	5
Curriculum coverage charts	6

The Crab Dragon
Guided or group reading	9
Group and independent reading activities	10
Speaking, listening and drama activities	12
Writing activities	12

No Tricks, Gran!
Guided or group reading	13
Group and independent reading activities	14
Speaking, listening and drama activities	15
Writing activities	16

Painting the Loft
Guided or group reading	17
Group and independent reading activities	18
Speaking, listening and drama activities	19
Writing activities	20

The Lost Chimp
Guided or group reading	21
Group and independent reading activities	22
Speaking, listening and drama activities	24
Writing activities	24

Green Planet Kids
Guided or group reading	25
Group and independent reading activities	26
Speaking, listening and drama activities	27
Writing activities	28

Crunch!
Guided or group reading	29
Group and independent reading activities	30
Speaking, listening and drama activities	32
Writing activities	32

Introduction

Welcome to *Floppy's Phonics!* This series gives you decodable phonic stories featuring all your favourite *Oxford Reading Tree* characters. The books provide the perfect opportunity for consolidation and practice of synthetic phonics within a familiar setting, to build your children's confidence. As well as having a strong phonic focus, each story is a truly satisfying read with lots of opportunities for comprehension, so they are fully in line with the simple view of reading.

Phonic development

The *Floppy's Phonics* Stage 4 stories support a synthetic phonics approach to early reading skills and are closely aligned to *Letters and Sounds*. They should be used for practice and consolidation. The books should be read in the suggested order (see chart on page 3), so that children can benefit from the controlled introduction, revision and consolidation of the phonemes. They can be used before the *Floppy's Phonics Non-fiction* books at the same stage. In addition, they can be used for practice and consolidation after introducing the sounds with other programmes.

The series can be used by children working within Phase 4 of *Letters and Sounds*, to support them as they broaden their knowledge of graphemes and phonemes for use in reading and spelling. The books will help to embed these vital early phonics skills, and help to ensure that children will experience success in learning to read and thus will be motivated to keep on reading.

Your children will benefit most from reading *Floppy's Phonics Stage 4* if they are able to:

- recognize the vowel digraphs from *Letters and Sounds* Phase 3
- recognize the *Letters and Sounds* high frequency words for Phases 3 and 4
- blend adjacent consonants occurring at the beginnings and ends of words
- read some phonically decodable two and three syllable words with increasing confidence

Phonic focus

This chart shows which phonemes are introduced and practised in each title.

Title	ORT Stage Book band colour Year group	*Letters and Sounds* phase	Phonic focus	Phonic focus revisited
The Crab Dragon	Stage 4 Blue Y1/ P2	Phase 4	initial, middle and final adjacent consonants	x, w, y, ch, sh, ng, th, ai, ee, igh, oo (short) ear, or, ar, air, ow, er, ure, oo (long)
No Tricks, Gran!	Stage 4 Blue Y1/ P2	Phase 4	initial and final adjacent consonants	y, x, w, j, qu, ng, ee, igh, oa, oo (long), oo (short), ur, ar, or, er
Painting the Loft	Stage 4 Blue Y1/ P2	Phase 4	initial, middle and final adjacent consonants polysyllabic words	ai, ee, igh, oo (short), ow, er, sh, ch
The Lost Chimp	Stage 4 Blue Y1/ P2	Phase 4	Initial, middle and final adjacent consonants polysyllabic words	w, j, y, ah, ch, th, ee, igh, oa, oo (long), oo (short), ar, ow, er, or
Green Planet Kids	Stage 4 Blue Y1/ P2	Phase 4	Initial and final adjacent consonants, polysyllabic words	sh, ss, ear, ll, ai, ee, oa, oo (short), ar, –er
Crunch!	Stage 4 Blue Y1/ P2	Phase 4	initial, middle and final adjacent consonants, polysyllabic words	ee, ar, ow, ear, sh, ck, oa, ch, th, ll

Phonic focus

Vocabulary

High frequency words are words which occur frequently in children's books. Many of them are decodable, some of them are "tricky". The words are defined in line with *Letters and Sounds*.

Decodable words

Most of the common words introduced in *Floppy's Phonics* are phonically decodable, using phonic skills and knowledge that is gradually developed through the series.

Tricky words

Tricky words are words which contain unusual grapheme-phoneme correspondences (e.g. *we, they*). The advice in *Letters and Sounds* is that children should be taught to recognize the phonemes they know within these words and to distinguish these from the tricky bits. For example, in the word *they*, children should be taught to recognize the grapheme *th* and then taught the tricky sound of 'ey' in this context.

High frequency words used in each book

The Crab Dragon	Decodable words	children, went, it's
	Tricky words	said, do, there, so, what, were
No Tricks, Gran!	Decodable words	children, just
	Tricky words	come, said, were, like, what, one
Painting the Loft	Decodable words	went, children, it's, just
	Tricky words	were, there, have, some, said, like, one
The Lost Chimp	Decodable words	just, help, went
	Tricky words	one, there, said, come, little, do, have, what, some
Green Planet Kids	Decodable words	help(ing), went
	Tricky words	were, there, said, what, some, one
Crunch!	Decodable words	children, went, just
	Tricky words	were, what, there, said, out, come, have, like, do

Comprehension Strategies

Reading is about making meaning, and it is particularly important that a child's earliest reading books offer opportunities for making meaning and telling a complete story. As with all *Oxford Reading Tree* stories, the titles in *Floppy's Phonics* are fun stories which children will really enjoy, and which will give you lots of scope for practising and extending their comprehension skills.

Story	Comprehension strategy taught through these Group/Guided Reading Notes				
	Prediction	Questioning	Clarifying	Summarizing	Imagining
The Crab Dragon	✓		✓	✓	✓
No Tricks, Gran!	✓	✓	✓		✓
Painting the Loft	✓		✓	✓	
The Lost Chimp	✓		✓	✓	✓
Green Planet Kids	✓	✓	✓	✓	✓
Crunch!	✓	✓	✓	✓	✓

Curriculum coverage charts

Key

C = Language comprehension   Y = Year   P = Primary
W = Word recognition   F = Foundation/Reception

In the designations such as 5.2, the first number represents the strand and the second number the individual objective

	Speaking, Listening, Drama	Reading	Writing
The Crab Dragon			
PNS Literacy Framework (Y1)	1.3 2.1, 2.2 3.1, 3.2, 3.3	**W** 5.4 **C** 6.2, 6.5, 7.2, 7.3, 7.4	9.1, 12.1, 12.2
National Curriculum	working within level 1		
Scotland (Curriculum for Excellence) (P2)	CfE First Level: LIT 110K, LIT 102B	CfE First Level: LIT 112N, LIT 113P, LIT 119U	CfE First Level: LIT 125AC
N. Ireland (P2)	1, 2, 5, 6, 8, 9, 10, 11	1, 2, 3, 4, 6, 8, 10, 11, 14, 15	1, 2, 3, 4, 6, 7, 10, 12, 13
Wales (Key Stage 1)	Range: 1, 3, 4 Skills: 2, 3, 4, 5 Lang Dev: 3	Range: 1, 2, 4, 5, 6 Skills: 1, 2 Lang Dev: 1, 2	Range: 2, 3, 4 Skills: 1, 2, 3, 4, 6, 7, 8, 9 Lang Dev: 1, 4
No Tricks, Gran!			
PNS Literacy Framework (Y1)	1.3 2.1, 2.2 3.1, 3.2, 3.3 4.1	**W** 5.4 **C** 6.1, 6.2, 7.2, 7.3, 8.2	9.4, 12.1, 12.2
National Curriculum	working within level 1		
Scotland (Curriculum for Excellence) (P1)	CfE First Level: LIT 107G	CfE First Level: LIT 112N, LIT 113P	CfE First Level: LIT 121Y
N. Ireland (P1)	1, 2, 5, 6, 7, 8, 9, 10, 11	1, 2, 3, 4, 6, 8, 10, 11, 14, 15	1, 2, 3, 4, 5, 6, 7, 10, 12, 13
Wales Key Stage 1	Range: 1, 3, 4 Skills: 2, 3, 4, 5 Lang Dev: 3	Range: 1, 2, 4, 5, 6 Skills: 1, 2 Lang Dev: 1, 2	Range: 2, 3, 4 Skills: 1, 2, 3, 4, 6, 7, 8, 9 Lang Dev: 1, 4

Curriculum coverage charts

	Speaking, Listening, Drama	Reading	Writing
Painting the Loft			
PNS Literacy Framework (Y1)	1.2, 1.3 2.1, 2.2 3.1, 3.2, 3.3	(W) 5.5 (C) 6.1, 6.5, 7.2, 7.3, 7.4	10.1, 12.1, 12.2
National Curriculum	working within level 1		
Scotland (Curriculum for Excellence) (P1)	CfE First Level: LIT 103C	CfE First Level: LIT 112N, LIT 113P, ENG 119V	CfE First Level: LIT 125AC
N. Ireland (P1)	1, 2, 5, 6, 8, 9, 10, 11	1, 2, 3, 4, 6, 8, 10, 11, 14, 15	1, 2, 3, 4, 6, 7, 10, 12, 13
Wales Key Stage 1	Range: 1, 3, 4 Skills: 2, 3, 4, 5 Lang Dev: 3	Range: 1, 2, 4, 5, 6 Skills: 1, 2 Lang Dev: 1, 2	Range: 2, 3, 4 Skills: 1, 2, 3, 4, 6, 7, 8, 9 Lang Dev: 1, 4
The Lost Chimp			
PNS Literacy Framework (Y1)	1.3 2.1, 2.2 3.1, 3.2, 3.3 4.2	(W) 5.3, 5.4 (C) 6.2, 7.1, 7.2, 7.3,	9.5, 12.1, 12.2
National Curriculum	working within level 1		
Scotland (Curriculum for Excellence) (P1)	CfE First Level: ENG 103C	CfE First Level: LIT 112N, LIT 113P, ENG 119V	CfE First Level: LIT 123AC
N. Ireland (P1)	1, 2, 5, 6, 7, 8, 9, 10, 11	1, 2, 3, 4, 6, 8, 10, 11, 14, 15	1, 2, 3, 4, 5, 6, 7, 10, 12, 13
Wales Key Stage 1	Range: 1, 3, 4 Skills: 2, 3, 4, 5 Lang Dev: 3	Range: 1, 2, 4, 5, 6 Skills: 1, 2 Lang Dev: 1, 2	Range: 2, 3, 4 Skills: 1, 2, 3, 4, 6, 7, 8, 9 Lang Dev: 1, 4

Curriculum coverage charts

	Speaking, Listening, Drama	Reading	Writing
Green Planet Kids			
PNS Literacy Framework (Y1)	1.3 2.1, 2.2 3.1, 3.2, 3.3 4.1	(W) 5.7 (C) 6.1, 6.3, 7.4, 7.2, 7.3	10.1, 12.1, 12.2
National Curriculum	working within level 1		
Scotland (Curriculum for Excellence) (P1)	CfE First Level: LIT 107G	CfE First Level: LIT 112N, LIT 113P, ENG 119V	CfE First Level: LIT 125AC
N. Ireland (P1)	1, 2, 5, 6, 7, 8, 9, 10, 11	1, 2, 3, 4, 6, 8, 10, 11, 14, 15	1, 2, 3, 4, 6, 7, 10, 12, 13
Wales Key Stage 1	Range: 1, 3, 4, 5 Skills: 2, 3, 4, 5 Lang Dev: 3	Range: 1, 2, 4, 5, 6 Skills: 1, 2 Lang Dev: 1, 2	Range: 2, 3, 4, 5 Skills: 1, 2, 3, 4, 6, 7, 8, 9 Lang Dev: 1, 4
Crunch!			
PNS Literacy Framework (Y1)	1.2, 1.3 2.1, 2.2 3.1, 3.2, 3.3	(W) 5.4, 5.5, 5.7 (C) 7.2, 7.3, 7.4	11.2, 12.1, 12.2
National Curriculum	working within level 1		
Scotland (Curriculum for Excellence) (P1)	CfE First Level: LIT 103C	CfE First Level: LIT 112N, LIT 113P, ENG 119V	CfE First Level: LIT 121Y
N. Ireland (P1)	1, 2, 5, 6, 7, 8, 9, 10, 11	1, 2, 3, 4, 6, 8, 10, 11, 14, 15	1, 2, 3, 4, 6, 7, 8, 10, 12, 13
Wales Key Stage 1	Range: 1, 3, 4, 5, 6 Skills: 2, 3, 4, 5 Lang Dev: 3	Range: 1, 2, 4, 5, 6 Skills: 1, 2 Lang Dev: 1, 2	Range: 2, 3, 4, 5 Skills: 1, 2, 3, 4, 6, 7, 8, 9 Lang Dev: 1, 4

The Crab Dragon

C = Language comprehension   **A** = Assessment
W = Word recognition   **O** = Objective

Guided or group reading

Phonic Focus:
Adjacent consonants used in this book include: br, dr, gr cr; bl, pl, fl; st, sp, sl, str; nn, tt, pp; –st, –nt, –nk

Phonemes revisited include: ai, ee, igh, oo (short), ear, or, ar, air, ow, er, ure, oo (long)

High frequency words: said, were, so, what, children, there, went, do, it's

Introducing the book

W Can children read the title? Help them to blend the adjacent consonants and read the title together: *The C-r-a-b D-r-a-g-o-n*

W Turn to page 1. Can children see adjacent consonants including 'r'? If children identify *park,* help them to recognize that the 'r' in *park* is part of the 'ar' grapheme, not an adjacent consonant.

C *(Predicting)* Encourage children to use prediction: *Do you think the dragon will win?*

- Look through the book, talking about what happens on each page. Use some of the high frequency words as you discuss the story (see chart on page 5).

Strategy check
Remind the children to sound the words out carefully, remembering that sometimes two letters can represent one sound. If they can't sound out a word, do they already know it from memory?

Independent reading
- Ask children to read the story aloud. Praise and encourage them while they read, and prompt as necessary.

The Crab Dragon

C *(Clarifying)* Ask children to tell you which dragon won. Do they think that it deserved to win?

Assessment Check that children:
- *(AF 1)* use phonic knowledge to sound out and blend the phonemes in words (see chart on page 3).
- *(AF 1)* distinguish adjacent consonants from consonants in vowel digraphs (e.g. *ar*) and trigraphs (e.g. *air*).
- *(AF 2 and 3)* use comprehension skills to work out what is happening.
- *(AF 1)* make a note of any difficulties the children encounter and of strategies they use to solve problems.

Returning to the text
W Which letters can come *second* in a pair of adjacent consonants?

Assessment *(AF 1)* Discuss any words the children found tricky and talk about strategies used.

Group and independent reading activities

Objective Segment words into their constituent phonemes in order to spell them correctly (6.2).

W **You will need:** flashcards showing the words: *crab, park, brill, flippers, green, hair, arm, sharp, ears, broom, beard, string, brown, winner*. Leave a small space between each letter when you write the words.

- Give each child a flashcard and a pair of scissors.
- Ask the children to cut the words up into phonemes (sounds).
- Remind them that adjacent consonants are two phonemes, so need to be cut into separate pieces.
- Then ask each child to hand the cut up word to another child. Can the second child rebuild the word?

Assessment *(AF 1)* Can children correctly identify the phonemes?

Objective Recognize automatically an increasing number of high frequency words (5.4).

The Crab Dragon

W In pairs, ask children to write as many words as they can which have two letters, the second of which is a vowel. Start them off with *to* and *be*.

- The children may find an alphabet strip useful.
- Check the number of words children have written. Possible words include: *do, go, no, so, to (ho-ho, ho, yo-yo); be, he, me, we; (la, ma, pa, ta)*
- Talk about the pronunciation of the vowel in each of the words the children suggest. Sort the *o* words into different pronunciations: *no, go, so; do to*.

Assessment *(AF 1)* Can children read the words automatically?

Objective To read and spell phonically decodable two syllable words (6.5).

W Check children's understanding of the word 'syllable'. Clarify that it means a 'beat' in a word. Orally, count how many syllables there are in *dragon, flipper, string, winner, Kipper, beard, better, children, picture.*

- Show children the words: *winner, flipper, Kipper, better.* Can children draw lines to show where the syllable boundary occurs? (*flip/per, Kip/per, bet/ter, win/ner*) It doesn't much matter if children put both middle consonants in one side or the other (*Ki/pper* or *Kipp/er*) as long as they recognize that before or after that consonant sound is the syllable boundary. Talk about the final sound in the words. Which letters represent that sound? (er)
- Show them the words *dragon, children, picture.* Can they draw the consonant boundaries in these words? (*dra/gon, child/ren, pic/ture*).
- Talk about how they decided where to draw the line in each word.

Assessment *(AF 1)* Can the children correctly identify the consonant boundary each time?

Objective Recognize the main elements that shape different texts (7.4).

C *(Summarizing)* Show three cards: beginning, middle, end.

- Ask children what happened at the beginning of the book.
- Ask what happened in the middle.
- Ask what happened at the end.
- Encourage discussion about how much of the story can be included under each of the headings.

The Crab Dragon

Assessment *(AF 4)* Can the children justify their separation of the story into the different parts?

Speaking, listening and drama activities

Objective Work effectively in groups (3.2).

- **C** *(Imagining)* Re-read the book, talking about the different stages of building a dragon and how the children co-operated to create the dragon.
- Look at all the other dragons in the pictures.
- Ask the children to work together to design a dragon. They can work with paper or construction materials.

Assessment Can the children work effectively in groups, listening to and appreciating the ideas of others?

Writing activities

Objective Draw on knowledge of texts in deciding what and how to write (9.1).

- **C** *(Clarifying)* Ask children to write about their dragon.
- They could draw and write labels and captions, write instructions to make the dragon, write a description of the dragon or explain how they made the dragon.
- Let the children choose how to write about their dragon.

Assessment *(Writing AF 2)* Can the children make appropriate choices about the language they use, given the mode of writing they have selected?

No Tricks, Gran!

C = Language comprehension **A** = Assessment
W = Word recognition **O** = Objective

Guided or group reading

Phonic Focus:
Adjacent consonants used in this book include: gr, cr, dr, tr, br; gl, bl; st, str, sn, sp, sl, pr; –st
Phonemes revisited include: ee, igh, oa, oo (long), oo (short), ur, ar, or, er
High frequency words: said, were, come, children, just, like, one, what

Introducing the book

W Can children read the title? Help them to blend the adjacent consonants and read the title together: *No T-r-i-ck-s, G-r-a-n*

C *(Clarifying)* Discuss the title, talking about the use of an exclamation mark at the end. Let the children practise reading the words, using the exclamation mark. When might someone say words in that way?

W Turn to page 1. Which pairs of adjacent consonants can the children identify? If the children do not pronounce the *g* in *ng*, help them to recognize that *ng* is not adjacent consonants because the two letters represent one sound.

C *(Predicting)* Encourage children to use prediction: *Why might someone say* "No Tricks, Gran!"?

• Look through the book, talking about what happens on each page. Use some of the high frequency words as you discuss the story (see chart on page 5).

Strategy check
Remind the children to sound the words out carefully, remembering that sometimes two letters can represent one sound. If they can't sound out a word, do they already know it from memory?

Independent reading

- Ask children to read the story aloud. Praise and encourage them while they read, and prompt as necessary.
- **(C)** *(Clarifying)* Ask children to tell you about the trick that Gran played.

Assessment Check that children:

- *(AF 1)* use phonic knowledge to sound out and blend the phonemes in words (see chart on page 3).
- *(AF 1)* distinguish adjacent consonants (e.g. *sp, sn*) from consonant digraphs (*sh, ch, th, ng*).
- *(AF 2 and 3)* use comprehension skills to work out what is happening.
- *(AF 1)* make a note of any difficulties the children encounter and of strategies they use to solve problems.

Returning to the text

(W) In this book, which letters follow *s* in adjacent consonants? (*st, sn, sp, str*)

Assessment *(AF 1)* Discuss any words the children found tricky and talk about strategies used.

Group and independent reading activities

Objective Spell new words using phonics as the prime approach (6.1).

(W) You will need: worksheets showing the words: *stop, long, glad, block, drag, truck, crack, crash, snap, branch, trip, step, much, this, and, drum, groan, tricks, rest, quick, spook, dress, night* written in large writing.

- On their worksheet, ask children to use one colour of pen to ring adjacent consonants – where you blend each of the consonants separately (e.g. *c-r*).
- They should use a second colour of pen to ring consonant digraphs – where two letters make one sound (e.g. *ch*).

Assessment *(AF 1)* Can children correctly distinguish adjacent consonants from consonant digraphs?

Objective Segment words into their constituent phonemes in order to spell them correctly (6.2).

(W) Can children make a list of all of the consonants they know which may double at the end of a word?
- Check that their list includes: *ff, ll, gg, dd, ss, zz, ck.*
- Ask them to write the words: *stuff, spill, frog, egg, glad, add, dress, quiz, frizz, black.*

Assessment *(AF 1)* Can children decide where to use double letters at the end of words?

Objective Recognize an increasing number of high frequency words (5.4).

(W) Let the children make a lotto game.
- They need to make one board each with six spaces and choose one word to write in each space. They can choose from: *said, were, come, children, just, like, one, it's, what.*
- If you write all of the words (three times each) on cards, you can shuffle the cards, then show children the words one at a time.
- The first child to read and call out the word correctly can claim the word and use it to cover the word on their lotto card.
- The first to cover all of the words on their card is the winner.

Assessment *(AF 1)* Can the children correctly read the words?

Objective Comment on characters, making imaginative links to their own experiences (8.2).

(C) *(Questioning)* Give each child a word and ask them to think about Gran in that way. Words could include: *fun, a nuisance, silly, boring, exciting.*
- Each child should re-read the book and find reasons to justify their response to Gran's behaviour.
- Let each of the children explain their reaction to Gran.

Assessment *(AF 4)* Can the children justify different responses to Gran's behaviour?

Speaking, listening and drama activities

Objective Explore familiar characters through role play (4.1).

(C) *(Questioning)* Think of questions to ask Gran about events in this book. Questions could focus around how Gran hurt her arm, why she gave the children a drum kit, why she played the trick, how she felt when Dad talked to her, how she feels about the children.

- Take turns in playing Gran and responding to the questions asked.

Assessment Can the children think of interesting questions and respond to questions in role?

Writing activities

Objective Create short simple texts on screen that combine words and images (9.4).

- *(Imagining)* Ask children to use a computer to write about the visit from Gran's point of view.
- They should use emoticons to show how Gran felt and what she did.

Assessment *(Writing AF 1)* Can the children use appropriate emoticons to show Gran's reactions at different points in the text?

Painting the Loft

C = Language comprehension A = Assessment
W = Word recognition O = Objective

Guided or group reading

Phonic Focus:

Adjacent consonants used in this book include:; -ft, -nt, -nd, -mp, -nk, -lf, -st; sl, fl, gr, st

Phonemes revisited include: ai, ee, igh, oo (short), ow, or, er, sh, ch

High frequency words: children, went, have, some, said, like, there, one, were, it's, just

Introducing the book

- **(W)** Can children read the title? Help them to identify the syllables and blend the adjacent consonants to read the title: *Paint-ing the L-o-f-t*
- **(W)** Turn to page 1. Which pairs of adjacent consonants can the children identify? Remind them that *ng* is not adjacent consonants. Can they explain why?
- **(C)** *(Predicting)* Encourage children to use prediction: *What are the children likely to do at Gran's?*
- Look through the book, talking about what happens on each page. Use some of the high frequency words as you discuss the story (see chart on page 5).

Strategy check

Remind the children to sound the words out carefully, remembering that sometimes two letters can represent one sound. If they can't sound out a word, do they already know it from memory?

Independent reading

- Ask children to read the story aloud. Praise and encourage them while they read, and prompt as necessary.
- *(Clarifying)* Ask children to tell you how the colours for the loft were chosen.

Assessment Check that children:

- *(AF 1)* use phonic knowledge to sound out and blend the phonemes in words (see chart on page 3).
- *(AF 1)* distinguish adjacent consonants (e.g. *lf, -pt*) from consonant digraphs (*sh, ch, th, ng*).
- *(AF 2 and 3)* use comprehension skills to work out what is happening.
- *(AF 1)* make a note of any difficulties the children encounter and of strategies they use to solve problems.

Returning to the text

(W) How many different adjacent consonants at the ends of words can children find?

Assessment *(AF 1)* Discuss any words the children found tricky and talk about strategies used.

Group and independent reading activities

Objective Apply phonic knowledge as the prime approach to reading unfamiliar words that are not completely decodable (5.5).

(W) Ask the children to look again at page 12. What did Gran bring for the children?

- Look at the word *blanket*. Talk about strategies for reading the word. Which bit is tricky? (*et*) Sound out the first syllable: *b-l-a-n-k* how can we use this word beginning, together with the context to work out the whole word?

Assessment *(AF 1)* Can children discuss the strategies they use for unfamiliar words?

Objective Read and spell new words using phonics as the prime approach (6.1).

(W) In secret, ask each child to write five words from the book. There should be consonants at the end of each word. The words should be written in large, clear, letters on strips of paper.

- Cut the words in two. The initial consonant or adjacent consonant together with the vowel should be on one side; the final adjacent consonants should be on the other (e.g. *pai-nt; lo-ft; bli-nk*).

Painting the Loft

- Children should mix up their cut-up words, then hand them to another child to make into complete words again.

Assessment *(AF 1)* Can children sound out and spell the word each time?

Objective Read and spell phonically decodable two and three syllable words (6.5).

- **W** Model spelling the word *plastic.* Be explicit about the strategy of first breaking the word into syllables, then sounding and spelling the first syllable before sounding out and spelling the second syllable.
- Ask the children to consider the word *silver.* Scaffold the experience while they try to spell it using the strategies you have just demonstrated.
- Repeat for *sticker, painting, going, children, blanket.*
- Each time, once the children have written the word, show them how to look at it again being aware of tricky bits and considering how to represent them (e.g. *blankit, or blanket?*).

Assessment *(AF 1)* Can the children correctly spell the words?

Objective Recognize the main elements that shape different texts (7.4).

- **C** *(Summarizing)* Re-read the book together.
- Give children a strip of paper with four boxes.
- Explain that they should draw a comic strip, showing the most important events in the story. Ask them to draw one event in each box.

Assessment *(AF 3)* Can the children identify the events which shape the story?

Speaking, listening and drama activities

Objective Re-tell stories, ordering events using story language (1.2).

- **C** *(Summarizing)* Explain that you want children to retell the story from the book.
- Show cue cards with time adverbials (*First, Later, After that, That evening, The next morning etc).* Talk about the use of these words and phrases in storytelling.

- Children will need their 'comic strip' as a visual cue while they plan their storytelling. Give them time to rehearse with their talking partner.
- Let each of the children present their story to the rest of the class.

Assessment *(AF4)* Can the children retell the events, sequencing them with appropriate storytelling language?

Writing activities

Objective Write chronological texts using simple structures (10.1).

C *(Summarizing)* Let children use their comic strips.

- Cut the strips up and ask children to retell the story in writing, writing one part under each picture.
- Remind them of the sequencing words and encourage the use of these words in their writing.

Assessment *(Writing AF 3)* Can the children organize the ideas successfully in a text?

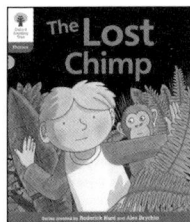

The Lost Chimp

> **C** = Language comprehension   **A** = Assessment
> **W** = Word recognition   **O** = Objective

Guided or group reading

Phonic Focus:
Adjacent consonants used in this book include: –ft, –pt, –xt, – st, –mp, –lf, –lk, –st, –nk, –nd–, –sp–, –il–; tr, fr, sl

Phonemes revisited include: ee, igh, oa, oo (long), oo (short), ar, ow, er, or

High frequency words: there, come, have, what, some, just, do, said, little, went, one, help

Introducing the book

W Can children read the title? Help them to blend the adjacent consonants and read the title together: *The L-o-s-t Ch-i-m-p*

W Turn to page 1. Which pairs of adjacent consonants can the children identify? Remind them that *th* and *sh* are not adjacent consonants. Can they explain why?

C *(Predicting)* Encourage children to use prediction: *How might Kipper lose a chimp?*

- Look through the book, talking about what happens on each page. Use some of the high frequency words as you discuss the story (see chart on page 5).

Strategy check

Remind the children to sound the words out carefully, remembering that sometimes two letters can represent one sound. If they can't sound out a word, do they already know it from memory?

Independent reading

- Ask children to read the story aloud. Praise and encourage them while they read, and prompt as necessary.

C *(Clarifying)* Ask children to tell you how Kipper lost his chimp.

Assessment Check that children:
- *(AF 1)* use phonic knowledge to sound out and blend the phonemes in words (see chart on page 3).
- *(AF 1)* distinguish adjacent consonants (e.g. *lf, -pt*) from consonant digraphs (*sh, ch, th, ng*).
- *(AF 2 and 3)* use comprehension skills to work out what is happening.
- *(AF 1)* make a note of any difficulties the children encounter and of strategies they use to solve problems.

Returning to the text

(W) How many different adjacent consonants at the ends of words can the children find?

Assessment *(AF 1)* Discuss any words the children found tricky and talk about strategies used.

Group and independent reading activities

Objective Segment words into their constituent phonemes in order to spell them correctly (6.2).

(W) You will need: magnetic letters.
- Secretly, select magnetic letters to spell a word with final adjacent consonants (e.g. *gift*).
- Put the letters, mixed up, on the table and ask children to sort them into a word.
- Talk about strategies for sorting the letters. Look at the combinations of consonants. Which could be initial adjacent consonants? And which could be final adjacent consonants?
- Let children take turns in selecting the letters to spell a word.

Assessment *(AF 1)* Can children correctly identify consonant combinations which might be final consonants?

Objective Identify the constituent parts of two and three syllable words (5.3).

W Look at the names and the types of animal that Kipper has: Amanda the panda, Casper the camel, Matilda the Mink, Thelma the owl, Linda and Imp the chimpanzees, Fred the frog, Sheena the shark.

- Ask children to clap the names and tell you how many syllables are in each.
- Show children the names. Can they draw lines to show the syllable boundaries in each one? It doesn't matter if the consonants are on a different side of the boundary than where you would draw them. Point out that each syllable must have a vowel sound.
- Discuss strategies for reading these longer words. If children need to sound out, they should sound out syllable by syllable, then blend the sounds in one syllable before moving on. (e.g. *ch-i-m-p chimp, a-n an, z-ee zee*) then they combine the syllables *chimp-an-zee, chimpanzee*.

Assessment *(AF 1)* Can children identify the syllable boundaries and combine syllables to read the words?

Objective Recognize automatically an increasing number of high frequency words (5.4).

W Introduce the high frequency words in the book.

- Identity the tricky bit of each word and talk about their spelling patterns.
- Introduce Shannon's Game. It's like Hangman except that in addition to guessing a letter, the children must also say where in the word the letter should go.
- Give the children a high frequency word and tell them they have 10 chances to work it out.
- Talk about the strategies they use to recognize the words.

Assessment *(AF 1)* Can the children correctly identify the words?

Objective Identify the main events in stories (7.1).

C *(Summarizing)* Ask children to tell you what happened in the story.

- Write each event on a piece of paper and give it to the children who suggested it. No child can have more than one event.
- When all of the children are holding their event, ask them to put themselves in the right order.

- Re-read the story both to check the events are in the right order and to check that no important events have been omitted.

Assessment *(AF 4)* Can the children identify main events correctly?

Speaking, listening and drama activities

Objective Act out their own story, using voices for characters (4.2).

- **(C)** *(Imagining)* Collect some soft toys in the classroom. Let the children work out a story for them, using the toys as characters.
- Once they have worked out a story, encourage them to rehearse it, thinking of voices for the characters.
- If possible, allow the children time to perform their story to the class and take pictures with a digital camera.

Assessment *(AF 3)* Can the children contribute to the invention and performance of a new story?

Writing activities

Objective Create short simple texts on paper or on screen, combining words with images (9.5).

- **(C)** *(Imagining)* Ask children to write the story they performed.
- If you took digital photos, let the children work on a computer, using the photos to illustrate the story.

Assessment *(Writing AF 1)* Can the children write a creative and interesting story?

Green Planet Kids

> **C** = Language comprehension **A** = Assessment
> **W** = Word recognition **O** = Objective

Guided or group reading

Phonic Focus:
Adjacent consonants used in this book include: thr, gr, dr, fr, pr, cr, tr, br, pl, sl, bl, cl, wh st; –lbs, –nk, –nd, –nt, –sp, –st, –ft, -lf, -xt, -et
Phonemes revisited include: ai, ee, oa, oo (short), ar, sh, ss, ear, ll, –er
High frequency words: were, there, some, said, one, what, they, went, help(ing)

Introducing the book

W Can children read the title? Help them to blend the adjacent consonants and read the title together: *G-r-ee-n P-l-a-n-e-t K-i-d-s*

W Turn to page 1. Which pairs of adjacent consonants can the children identify? Remind them that *ng* is not a pair of adjacent consonants. Can they explain why?

C *(Predicting)* Encourage children to use prediction: *What kinds of things might the Green Planet Kids do?*

- Look through the book, talking about what happens on each page. Use some of the high frequency words as you discuss the story (see chart on page 5).

Strategy check
Remind the children to sound the words out carefully, remembering that sometimes two letters can represent one sound. If they can't sound out a word, do they already know it from memory?

Independent reading

- Ask children to read the story aloud. Praise and encourage them while they read, and prompt as necessary.

C *(Clarifying)* Ask the children to tell you what the Green Planet kids do.

Assessment Check that children:
- *(AF 1)* use phonic knowledge to sound out and blend the phonemes in words (see chart on page 3).
- *(AF 1)* distinguish adjacent consonants (e.g. *lf, -pt*) from consonant digraphs (*sh, ch, th, ng*).
- *(AF 2 and 3)* use comprehension skills to work out what is happening.
- *(AF 1)* make a note of any difficulties the children encounter and of strategies they use to solve problems.

Returning to the text

(W) How many different adjacent consonants at the ends of words can children find?

Assessment *(AF 1)* Discuss any words the children found tricky and talk about strategies used.

Group and independent reading activities

Objective Identify the constituent parts of two syllable and three syllable words (6.3).

(W) Ask children how they would recognize a word that has more than one syllable.
- How many words in the book can they find with two or three syllables.
- Help the children to group the words they find:
  o Compound words: *Toadstool, into*
  o Words with *ing* and *er* endings: *helping, deeper*
  o Words with more than one syllable: *planet, plastic, packet, metal, Wilma, animals, children, under*

Assessment *(AF 1)* Can children correctly identify words with more than one syllable?

Objective Spell new words using phonics as the prime approach (6.1).

(W) Say some of the words from the book and ask children to write them down in a list e.g. *bench, drink, crisp, black, junk, drum, mend, paint, rust, plan.*

- In pairs ask children to think of another word to write beside each of the words you suggested. The new word should either begin or end with the same consonant or adjacent consonants as the first word e.g. *bench – ball* or *bench – lunch; drink – drain* or *drink – pink; crisp – crab* or *crisp – wisp* etc.

Assessment *(AF 1)* Can children sound out and spell the new word each time?

Objective Read and spell phonically decodable two and three syllable words (5.7).

- **(W)** Model spelling the word *Toadstool.* Be explicit about the strategy of first breaking the word into syllables, then sounding out and spelling the first syllable before sounding out and spelling the second syllable.
- Ask the children to consider the word *children.* Scaffold the experience while they try to spell it using the strategies you have just demonstrated.
- Repeat for *animals, plastic, packet, metal, under.*
- Each time, once the children have written the word, show them how to look at it again being aware of the tricky bits and considering how to represent them (e.g. *metel,* or *metal?*).

Assessment *(AF 1)* Can the children correctly spell the words?

Objective Identify the main characters in stories (7.1).

- **(C)** *(Questioning)* Give the children question starters *how* and *why*. Can they all think of a question for one of the characters in the book which begins with one of those words?
- Distinguish between 'it's there' questions – where the answer is in the text or the pictures – and 'what do you think' questions which involve more thought. Encourage children to ask at least one 'what do you think' question.

Assessment *(AF 3)* Can the children frame 'what do you think' questions?

Speaking, listening and drama activities

Objective Explore familiar characters through improvisation and role play (4.1).

- **(C)** *(Imagining)* Re-read the book together, to reinforce the events and actions in the story. Let each child focus on a character they are particularly interested in.

Green Planet Kids

- Let children take turns to be one of the characters in the story. In role, they should answer the questions of the others.

Assessment *(AF 2)* Can the children improvise good answers to the questions and demonstrate good understanding of the events in the book?

Writing activities

Objective Write chronological texts using simple structures (10.1).

C *(Summarizing)* Ask the children to write a newspaper account of what the Green Planet Kids achieved in the wood.

Assessment *(Writing AF 3)* Can the children organize the ideas successfully in a text?

Crunch!

> **C** = Language comprehension **A** = Assessment
> **W** = Word recognition **O** = Objective

Guided or group reading

Phonic Focus:
Adjacent consonants used in this book include: tr, gr, pr, cr, dr, str, scr, cl, gl, pl, st, nt, fr, -pt, -st, -nt, -sk, -nk, -nd, -mp, -lk

Phonemes revisited include: ee, ar, ow, ear, sh, ck, oa, ch, th, ll

High frequency words: children, were, what, there, just, come, have, like, said, out, do, went

Introducing the book

W Can children read the title? Help them to blend the adjacent consonants to read the title: *C-r-u-n -ch!*

C *(Clarifying)* Talk about the exclamation mark. What does it tell the reader about how to say the word?

W Turn to page 1. Which pairs of adjacent consonants can the children identify? Remind them that *ch, sh* and *ng* are not adjacent consonants. Can they explain why?

C *(Predicting)* Encourage children to use prediction: *What might go* crunch!*?*

- Look through the book, talking about what happens on each page. Use some of the high frequency words as you discuss the story (see chart on page 5).

Strategy check
Remind the children to sound the words out carefully, remembering that sometimes two letters can represent one sound. If they can't sound out a word, do they already know it from memory?

Independent reading
- Ask children to read the story aloud. Praise and encourage them while they read, and prompt as necessary.

(C) *(Clarifying)* Ask children to tell you how the children got to know Greg.

Assessment Check that children:
- *(AF 1)* use phonic knowledge to sound out and blend the phonemes in words (see chart on page 3).
- *(AF 1)* distinguish adjacent consonants (e.g. *lf, -pt*) from consonant digraphs (*sh, ch, th, ng*).
- *(AF 2 and 3)* use comprehension skills to work out what is happening.
- *(AF 1)* make a note of any difficulties the children encounter and of strategies they use to solve problems.

Returning to the text

(W) How many words with two sets of adjacent consonants can the children find (e.g. *cr-a-sh*)?

Assessment *(AF 1)* Discuss any words the children found tricky and talk about strategies used.

Group and independent reading activities

Objective Read and spell phonically decodable two syllable and three syllable words (5.7).

(W) Show children a two syllable word from the book (e.g. *shopping, present, traffic, electric, glinting, windscreen*).
- Talk about the word. Do the children recognize it or do they need to sound it out? Are there any tricky bits? Which strategies can they use to work out the tricky bits?
- Once you have looked at a word for reading, ask children to spell it. Again, discuss strategies of segmenting the words into syllables and phonemes in order to spell them correctly.
- Talk about the tricky bits and strategies for working them out.

Assessment *(AF 1)* Can children use a range of strategies to read and spell the words?

Objective Apply phonic knowledge and skills as the prime approach to reading (5.5).

(W) Write one syllable words with two sets of adjacent consonants (e.g. *crunch, crept, glint, drink*) on strips of paper.

Crunch!

- Cut the words up so that you have a mixture of adjacent consonants and vowels.
- Can the children identify which sets of adjacent consonants must be word final (e.g. *nch, pt, nt, nk*) and which can only be word initial (*dr, cr, gl*). Can they think of any adjacent consonants which can be either? (*sp, st* and *sk*).
- Put the word pieces in three piles: beginning, middle, end. Randomly pick one piece from each pile to make a nonsense word. Ask children to silently sound out and then read the nonsense word.

Assessment *(AF 1)* Can children accurately sound out and read the word each time?

Objective Recognize automatically an increasing number of familiar high frequency words (5.4).

- Make pairs of high frequency words that have something in common. E.g. *some, come; so, no; do, to; were, there; when, what; like, have.*
- Ask children to tell you what is the same and what is different each time. E.g. *some* and *come* rhyme and look the same except for the *s* and the *c*. The tricky bits in both words are the *o* that sounds like /u/ and the *e* which doesn't make any sound.
- *Were* and *there* look like they should rhyme, but they don't. In both words the *ere* is the tricky bit because it doesn't sounds as it looks.
- Continue to identify similarities, differences and tricky bits in pairs of words. Looking carefully at the words and explaining them like this will help children to know and recognize the words.

Assessment *(AF 1)* Can the children identify similarities, differences and tricky bits in each pair of words?

Objective Identify the main events in the story (7.4).

- *(Summarizing)* Re-read the book together.
- Give each child a piece of paper and ask them to draw the most important or interesting event in the book.
- Clarify that the answer will be different for different children, so each child will have to think for themselves.

Crunch!

- When they have finished, encourage the children to talk to the rest of the group about why they chose this particular event.

Assessment *(AF 3)* Can the children select an appropriate event and justify it?

Speaking, listening and drama activities

Objective Re-tell stories, ordering events using story language (1.2).

- **C** *(Questioning)* Re-read the book to establish the events in the children's minds.
- Put a policeman's hat on one child – or an armband saying 'POLICE'
- Ask the child to imagine that they are a police officer who has heard, but not seen, the crash. The police officer should interview the characters to find out what happened and what might happen next.

Assessment *(AF 3)* Can the children ask and answer questions in role?

Writing activities

Objective Use capital letters and full stops when punctuating simple sentences (11.2).

- **C** *(Imagining)* Prepare a writing frame on the computer for children to write into.
- The writing frame should be presented like a police report with space to write the character's name, together with what they saw, heard and did.
- Let children select any character and complete their police report, adding any details which seem relevant.

Assessment *(Writing AF 6)* Can the children punctuate their writing correctly?